Man on the Moon

by Anastasia Suen • *illustrated by* Benrei Huang

PUFFIN BOOKS

For my family,
who encouraged me to follow my dreams;
and for all the people at NASA who
made the dream a reality
—A.C.S.

To my son, Shane,
for leading me on the incredible journey
of motherhood
—B.H.

PUFFIN BOOKS
Published by the Penguin Group
Penguin Putnam Books for Young Readers,
345 Hudson Street, New York, New York 10014, U.S.A.
Penguin Books Ltd, 27 Wrights Lane, London W8 5TZ, England
Penguin Books Australia Ltd, Ringwood, Victoria, Australia
Penguin Books Canada Ltd, 10 Alcorn Avenue, Toronto, Ontario, Canada M4V 3B2
Penguin Books (N.Z.) Ltd, 182-190 Wairau Road, Auckland 10, New Zealand

Penguin Books Ltd, Registered Offices: Harmondsworth, Middlesex, England

First published in the United States of America by Viking, a member of Penguin Putnam Inc,. 1997
Published by Puffin Books, a division of Penguin Putnam Books for Young Readers, 2002

19 20

Text copyright © Anastasia Suen, 1997
Illustrations copyright © Benrei Huang, 1997
All rights reserved

THE LIBRARY OF CONGRESS HAS CATALOGED THE VIKING EDITION AS FOLLOWS:
Suen, Anastasia.
Man on the moon / by Anastasia Suen ; illustrated by Benrei Huang.
p. cm.
Summary: Describes in illustrations and simple text the Apollo 11 mission to the moon,
culminating in man's first lunar landing.
ISBN: 0-670-87393-4 (hc)
1. Project Apollo (U.S)—Juvenile literature. [1. Project Apollo (U.S.) 2. Apollo 11 (Spacecraft)
3. Space flight to the moon.]
I. Huang, Benrei, ill. II. Title.
TL789.8.U62A667 1997 629.45′4′0973—dc21 97-2628 CIP AC

Puffin Books ISBN 978-0-14-056598-0

Printed in the United States of America

Moon,
do you remember
your first visitors?

It was 1969 . . .

Astronauts Collins, Aldrin, and Armstrong
suited up.

Each had flown in space,
but no one had *ever* touched the moon.
No one.

Some said it couldn't be done.
Astronauts Collins, Aldrin, and Armstrong
were going to try.

Into *Apollo 11* they climbed.
The countdown began.
3–2–1 and . . .

"Liftoff! Liftoff!
Apollo 11
has cleared the tower!"

Saturn 5
shot them
into the sky.

Around the Earth they flew
as the rockets dropped off,
then *whoosh!* straight for the moon. . . .

Hours and days passed.
The people on Earth
watched the astronauts on TV.

Over and over
the capsule turned.
Suddenly, the sky went dark.

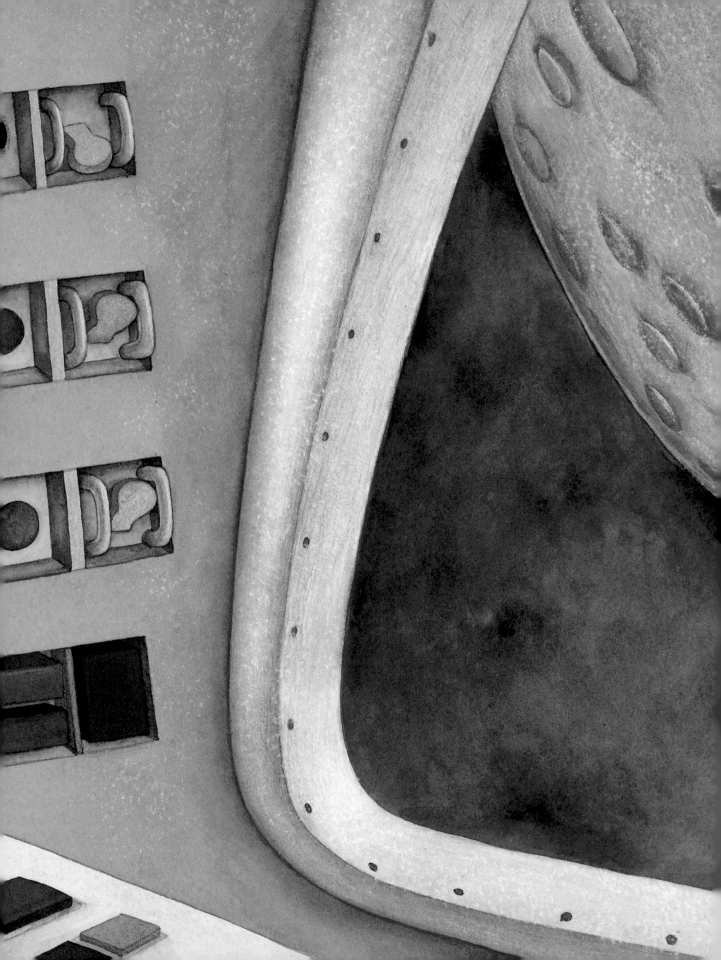

It was the moon!
For the first time,
Apollo 11 saw the moon.

The astronauts circled,
looking for a place to land.
In the morning,
their spacecraft would separate.

Columbia, named after Columbus,
would sail around the moon.
The *Eagle*, like a bird, would fly there.

The next day,
Aldrin and Armstrong
climbed into the *Eagle*.

Collins, in *Columbia*,
pressed a button,
and off the *Eagle* flew. . . .

Buttons and gadgets,
switches and lights!
Alarms rang again and again.

In the control room,
Houston said, "Go."
The *Eagle* flew on.

On the moon,
craters loomed.
The *Eagle* was going too fast!

Armstrong took the controls
and began to fly.
Houston and the Earth waited.

Fifty feet
Thirty feet
Contact!

"Houston,
Tranquility Base here.
The *Eagle* has landed."

With cameras rolling,
as millions watched,
Astronaut Neil Armstrong touched the moon.

"That's one small step for man,"
he said,
"one giant leap for mankind."

Aldrin and Armstrong
took pictures, collected rocks,
and planted the American flag.

Hours later,
the *Eagle* left the moon
and linked up with *Columbia*.

Home again,
Collins, Aldrin, and Armstrong
splashed down in the Pacific Ocean.

Some said it couldn't be done.
Mike Collins, Buzz Aldrin, and Neil Armstrong
proved them wrong . . .

and made history.

> **HERE MEN FROM THE PLANET EARTH**
> **FIRST SET FOOT ON THE MOON**
> **JULY 1969, A.D.**
> **WE CAME IN PEACE FOR ALL MANKIND.**

(*Plaque left on the moon by* **Apollo 11**)

AUTHOR'S NOTE

I was three when we moved to Florida. It was 1959, the year NASA selected the first astronauts. My father worked at Cape Canaveral. He sailed on missile-tracking ships, all the way down to Africa.

I grew up with NASA. My brother and I watched the launches on our black-and-white TV and then ran out into the backyard to see the ball of fire rise, rise, rise into the sky. We watched until it disappeared.

When I went to school, everyone would stand on the school's front lawn to watch the sky on launch days. We saw that ball of flame rise, and we knew a man was inside. Someday, a man would go to the moon. President Kennedy said so.

Ten years later, I sat in front of another television set, in California. I was thirteen now, and although President Kennedy was gone, his promise was about to come true. Around the world, millions of people held moonwatch parties and watched TV. We watched as the *Eagle*'s camera began to roll. We sat, transfixed, as Neil Armstrong stepped out onto the moon.

"That's one small step for man," he said, "one giant leap for mankind."

And it was. . . .

Footnote: A word was lost from the transmission when Neil Armstrong first stepped onto the moon. No one knows why. What we were supposed to hear was: "That's one small step for *a* man, one giant leap for mankind."

—*Anastasia Suen*